How to Make
Bad Things Happen to
Awful People

How to Make
Bad Things Happen
to Awful People

Spells for Revenge, Power & Protection

DEBORAH GRAY

HAMPTON ROADS

Cover and text design Kathryn Sky-Peck
Using Ilustrations by Lilla Bölecz

Hampton Roads Publishing Company, Inc.
Charlottesville, VA 22906
Distributed by Red Wheel/Weiser, LLC
www.redwheelweiser.com

Sign up for our newsletter and special offers by going to
www.redwheelweiser.com/newsletter/

ISBN: 978-1-57174-848-5

Library of Congress Cataloging-in-Publication Data available upon request.

Printed in Canada

MAR

10 9 8 7 6 5 4 3 2 1

CONTENTS

Introduction

You deserve
to be protected
be a winner
and be avenged!

Life is beautiful ... but crossing paths with awful people can make your life a misery.

Let's face it: some people are just horrible beasts.

Why not live your life free from stress—while getting back at that love rat who dumped you or the toady traitor who sabotaged your dreams?

Revenge may not be sweet, but it sure packs a punch against your enemies.

Don't just get mad, get even

Time to throw out the painful past and win back your pride and passion for the future.

So get yourself armed and charmed with the humorous hexes, protection spells, and banishing incantations within this book. Get your mojo back on the scoundrels who have sabotaged your dreams—then learn to laugh out loud again while regaining your personal power.

And don't worry, while you are stirring up the hocus pocus to move things in your favor, these cheeky charms won't cause any real damage.

Actually it can be great karma to magically influence a repeat offender to wake up to their heinous behavior—before they go on to inflict even worse treachery on their next victim.

No horrible beasts have been harmed during the casting of these spells

(of course, there is no guarantee that they won't feel the cold winds of change blowing around them).

Rest assured, with this level of expert witchy advice, any unforeseen journeys into the cruel, cold side of life will soon become a little easier to handle.

CHAPTER ONE

History of Hexing

Hexing is not new. In fact it's a classical part of our world history. Despite going underground for a time in the middle ages, witchery has never really wavered in popularity.

The human need for rituals of revenge is as old as time itself and has been documented since the beginning of the written word.

During the times of Julius Caesar, the people of Rome took to their revered places of worship with sheets of malleable lead and scribbled upon them incantations of protection and revenge over their foes.

After sliding the softened metallic notes to the Gods into the sacred walls of their temples, they often would finish off these folk-charmed events with a celebratory banquet themed on the certainty that, despite doing nothing illegal or actually committing an act of physical violence, revenge on their personal wrongdoers was inevitable—if not sooner, then definitely later.

The Ancient Greeks, centuries before the Romans, also knew that the universal forces—or as they liked to call them, the Gods of the Pantheon—were connected to our human consciousness and therefore connected to our past, present, and future psychological health.

Those old philosophers and writers of the texts of Hellenic wisdom, along with the Druid masters within all the ancient Celtic lands and many other cultures of old, allowed that rituals were a door into understanding the natural and supernatural world around us. Importantly, ritual was also a way of averting disasters and attaining a sense of control over our destiny—even if all they attained was a *feeling* of being in control.

Wise ones, magicians, astrologers, high priests and priestesses, all the pagan world scholars usually practiced sorcery. Being great observers of nature and human behavior, they categorized everything around them in lists of their corresponding magical and medicinal meanings. Corresponding magic is based on the belief that each plant, animal, season, and stage of the sun and moon had unique but universally aligned aspects which, if understood and directed toward a purpose, could be used as a ritual tool for hundreds of different spells of fertility, love, success, and revenge.

The philosophers and the magicians of many cultures around the world knew that human power begins in the brain.

*Hexing can be great
for your health—
fighting back is vital!*

It was essential that their minds, usually so crowded with anxious thoughts and instinctual fears, could be switched off by ritual when needed, in order to heal from the daily bumps and battles and to get on with the practical day-to-day of material life.

Hexing can be great for your health—fighting back is vital!

Holding on to resentment or allowing people to hurt you also means you are enabling them to go on hurting other people as well.

A protection spell can actually do a lot of good by speeding up important life lessons. Obsessing over the pain of treachery can lead you to become fearful of partaking in everything that life has to offer, therefore missing out on future happiness. That's where a magical dash of delicious vengeance can really hit the spot and turn any sad, tortured memories around.

As Shakespeare said,

Grief softens the mind.

Think therefore on revenge and Cease to Weep!

Of course, actually committing acts of vigilante style revenge is neither advisable nor legal. After all, what is the point of getting up close and physically angry with someone, and then ending up worse off than before? You may even lose your job or get shunned by your friends and family. So, what is the solution? This is where turning your pain around through the virtual quantum world of magic comes in so handy.

Basically you get all of the delight of the privately experienced payback—without it swinging back onto you.

CHAPTER TWO

What About Manipulation?

Witches have been casting spells of love, stirring up healing potions and good-luck charms, casting astrology charts and performing readings, looking into our past and future for millennia.

The language of old magic is as varied and fascinating as the hundreds of cultures that have embraced its spell.

Sorcerers of all eras and persuasions practice magically weaving and bending time and space in their own way and to cause changes within themselves through rituals of self-exploration.

The magic within these pages is based not upon casting spells to control others or to become master/mistress over someone else's life, but instead to look at empathic connections between all of us that can be empowered and protected against when needed to create changes within ourselves and to positively affect the world around us.

This in essence is the meaning of the ancient term *wicce* or "wicca"; this word also means "bending and weaving."

Now If someone wants to classify this magical craft of "bending and weaving" as manipulation, they are only half right because it's actually your *own* thoughts and your empathic connection with the universe you are "bending and weaving."

You see, the entire cosmos—including you, your mind, body, and spirit—is universally connected. We are all made of energy. Everything around us is also the physical manifestation of thought, and your thoughts have the power to change the atmosphere of your mind and soothe or excite your emotions, which in turn may also change the dynamic of the atmosphere around you.

The genuine study of magic is about looking behind the veil of the mysteries of our universe, without superstition or simple theatrics, and keeping within a scientific and philosophical approach—and of course, not forgetting your sense of humor.

For centuries, there has been an underlying fear, a kind of myth and distorted perception, that one could take over another person's "free will" by, for instance, casting a love spell on them. That kind of thinking is one of the main reasons spellcasters were persecuted in the past, but it's really just a lot of superstition left over from the Dark Ages. A magic spell performed correctly can certainly change the atmosphere and greatly alter the dynamic flow—the energy patterns—between two or more people, which in itself is an incredible feat. But a person's final decision and ultimate choice is always made according to their own free will and universal destiny, and that just can't be taken away by or replaced with a spell.

You see, a lot of logic also comes into the study of magic, and if you are really interested in the inner lore of higher-minded magic, then the following is important to think about.

The universe endows us with the gift of free will so that we have the ultimate choice and responsibility for our own lives.

Our free will is one of our greatest powers. It gives us the ability to shape our own lives and futures, and a magic spell or any other enchantment cannot take away a person's free will.

Don't all spells have to follow the rede and the law of return?

Contrary to what you may have previously read, the mod-ern forms of rules and redes are not learned from ancient religious texts or old "witches" laws or from any known ancient practice of the Craft. They are primarily a 20th-century invention. There are a lot of different opinions about what is "good" and what is "bad," or manipulative, magic. People also speak often about the "laws of three-fold return." Quite a few paths within the Craft have their own rules—what they call "redes"—but these are more like guides or suggestions for "higher-minded" behavior and are not absolute laws of witches or spells. You will often see the phrases such as "as it harm none, do as thou will" and "the Law of threefold return" written into many modern books on magic and wicca. These popular phrases weren't actually derived from ancient writings of old Celtic origin or even from any original traditions of old magic; they are symbolic terms that have been adapted from a variety of different sources and cultures, including Buddhism and Freemasonry, merged with new traditions adapted by a few of the more popular modern-age authors and teachers who went on to build their own way of thinking and writing on the subject during the second half of the 20th century.

If you would like to feel confident you are performing magic correctly, then before you cast your spells or perform a ritual, follow these steps:

• Spend time looking into your inner self

• Meditate on you inner spiritual and emotional awareness

• Then start to bring into focus your intent and purpose of the spell or ritual you are about to perform.

The most genuine and lasting forms of magical power come from within a well-balanced and observant point of view.

The essence of magic should always feel inspiring to you; it is super empowered by flowing through a free and uninhibited sense of inner spirit.

This is a spiritual path as well as a philosophy, a way of looking at science, mathematics, nature, and the universe.

All combined, it is an ancient path; but it is also a path of modern knowledge that can help us understand the past and feel ready for future events.

To be a balanced magical being is an ever-evolving spiritual path that travels side by side with science, our physical health, our environment on earth, as well as our healthy skepticism. It's also about becoming capable of understanding and handling anything you set your mind to and, very importantly, allowing your neighbor their freedom to do the same.

DEMONS OR DIAMONDS

Don't worry, modern spellcasting is not about trying to raise up nasty ghouls or zombies or vampires. Because even if you wanted to waste your time trying, you'd have more chance of

turning a fake sparkler into a diamond than raising even one annoying dust mite.

The old legends and fear of magic are left over from the days of religious persecution, when anyone who was even remotely an alternative thinker was labeled as a heretic and accused of trying to invoke spirits and evil goblins.

The Hollywood-style wiccacraft that you see in films and TV shows is very entertaining, but it's all hocus-pocus, the product of a scriptwriter's vivid imagination. Yes, of course there are inspiring forces of nature zooming around the metaphysical plane. Nature's energy is all around and within us, and most of superstition is due to our inner fears. Yet everyone on Earth lives side by side with the whole spectrum of incredible energies and powers on a daily basis without thinking twice about it.

Next time you glimpse the sun through some clouds, walk by the sea, or get caught in a thunderstorm, just think about how much amazing power and energy there is right here in our everyday lives. Before we humans started to understand the science of things and discovered the laws of physics, natural phenomena like these were thought of as fearful gods to be kept at bay and given human names like

Thor the god of Thunder, Amon Ra the Sun god, and Neptune the Lord of the Sea.

Of course we now know that these "supernatural" forces are not actually "from the otherworld"; these elements are just another dimension of the whole picture of Nature—many of which were given names and human personalities by ancient civilizations in order to better understand, observe, and be respectful of all these very natural phenomena.

So try to abandon any superstitions or fears before you start spellcasting and performing rituals. The study of magic should allow you to open up to the possibilities of the natural universe and encourage your own human and spiritual development. The study of magic can also connect you with your instinctual being, wherein lies your own built-in protective system—the uncanny awareness of the level of your deep understanding and what you can and can't cope with.

Always trust in your own connection with the universe and your own instincts.

CHAPTER THREE

Waking Up the Witch

It's time to wake up your inner witch so you can do all of this fun stuff I like to call "voodoo therapy" or "sorcery for stress" without feeling uptight about it. This chapter will give you some basic spellcasting tools and techniques to help you keep a balanced view of the situation.

You can release any fears and know it's actually all about the intent and purpose of your spell: like self-defense, protection, resolving grief and heartache, and a whole lot of healing the inner you.

Let's face it, don't we all deserve to be wild and wikid for a day?

'Cause it sure feels so incredibly good to blow away those cobwebs and let it all go.

To prepare yourself for magic, use the light spiral technique described in the next section to help focus and raise energy. It will make you feel grounded and focused, but it isn't entirely essential. What you choose to do depends on your own instincts, preference, or traditions.

There are countless ways to raise energy. Some traditions cast their circle by calling up the four elements and the "Watchtowers," and then may raise up a "cone of power," while others believe in calling on protective spirits or angelic energies. Others again like to work with fairy or "Faery" energies or Nature sprites or the different pantheons of ancient gods and goddesses.

Whatever methods you use, work at your own pace and try out different approaches one at a time to see what works—what "resonates" magically for you. What works for you will often depend on what type of person you are. Maybe you are more of a cerebral type of person who feels more inspired by being alone or sitting in a circle with others, quietly focusing your mind and body with meditative rituals. Or you may get a lot of excitement and magical value from trying out the more physically involved rituals that incorporate dancing, beating drums, singing, and chanting (which can be done both alone or with a magical group).

Especially when you are just starting out in the Craft, it's best to keep it simple; there are easy circle castings that can help you connect with the "oneness" of yourself and the eternal universe.

LIGHT SPIRAL

This wonderful ritual is one of my favorite ways of casting a circle and raising a spiral of energy. It is for focusing and invoking a sense of growth and protection. It can help put you into a meditative and responsive state wherever you are and connect around, above, and below you. It requires no external tools but is still one of the most powerful and ancient rituals you can do. Perform it day or night, including whenever you feel your psychic and physical energies need a boost, or to enhance the power of a spell.

- Find a comfortable and private space, either outdoors or in-doors, and stand, breathing calmly. Loosely cup your hands together in front of you so that you can see the palms of both of your hands.

- Look closely at the center of both of your hands and look at the tiny lines on your palms. Observe how there appears to be a curved space that is perfect for holding a small sphere.

- Keep looking until you visualize that small sphere softly glowing in your hands and in your mind's eye. Imagine that it contains a miniuniverse that is shimmering with thousands, then millions, of tiny suns and stars, which are starting to merge into a minigalaxy of light.

- The more you look into this cosmic sphere, the more you really see this miniuniverse that has its own galaxy of stars circling slowly around inside it in a clockwise (right-turning) direction.

- Feel the power and energy of that minigalaxy as it starts to spiral up through your entire body.

- When you are feeling uplifted and revitalized, start turning on the spot to the right, in a clockwise direction.

- Spin once or twice in a circle and joyously fling the light sphere away from you and watch the sphere dissolve into the atmosphere, scattering those thousands of tiny stars that surround you with your own expanding galaxy and circle of light.

In the above spiral of light, you turn to the right because the right spiral is an ancient symbol and psychological trigger for going forward and moving toward the light. Think about the old saying "put your right foot forward" and why in most cultures we greet each other by shaking the right hand. Even our clocks, our precious timekeepers, turn "clockwise" to the right, and no

23

matter where you are on Earth, if you stand facing the North at dawn, the first life-giving rays of the sun will rise in the East and shine on your right side.

Because the sun's energy gives us light and life, humans, plants, and most other living creatures naturally turn toward the sunlight to "wake up," grow, and blossom.

The moon, on the other hand, is a cold and mysterious orb with a "dark" side. The left spiral, turning in the opposite direction toward the moon and night, helps us dream, rest, and travel through the more mysterious side of ourselves.

Through both evolution and culture, this "sunwise" and "moonwise"—right and left action—became a very strong part of the belief system. Throughout Europe and in many other parts of the world, right-turning, clockwise rituals like the one above have been performed for thousands of years and are magically effective in the most universal and profound way. There are some left-handed and Southern Hemisphere witches who prefer casting "forward motion" and "attraction" circles in an counterclockwise "widdershins" direction. And hey, that is perfectly cool if it works for them, but I personally wouldn't recommend you cast a "forward"

circle in a counterclockwise direction, regardless of what country or hemisphere you might be working in. Not because anything drastic can happen, but simply because our genetic and psychological adherence to these left and right actions is often too ingrained, and it can get confusing to swap around.

The left-hand side has received a bit of bad publicity in times gone by. Many natural left-handers were forced to write with their right hands. Even the word "sinister" is from the Latin word for "left"—*sinistra*—which later took on the meaning of "dark" and "evil." But this is just superstition, and casting a counterclockwise circle to trigger your left side does not have such a purely negative connotation in magic. It is about subconsciously turning to the direction of the moon and the night. The counterclockwise circle is cast for going backward into the past, for cleansing a space, or ridding yourself of leftover stress, or working with the deep and more mysterious witchy energies and your moonshadow side for a change.

Left-Hand Ritual

The widdershins, counterclockwise ritual, can be used for clearing away negative energies and past worries and for "washing" a magical space in readiness for further spellcasting and rituals.

- To begin, instead of visualizing a sphere of light, imagine you are holding a bowl of water. And as you look into it, start breathing deeply in and out.

- With each breath, imagine the water is drawing out all your self-doubt and fears about yourself.

- As it absorbs those heavy and negative sensations, feel the water revitalize you and recharge you with a sense of inner calm and strength.

- Whenever you are ready, start spinning to the left, in a counterclockwise direction, flinging the imaginary bowl of water away from you.

- Watch it flow into a beautiful velvety river of energy that dissolves into the atmosphere, washing over everything with a deep sense of spiritual cleansing and a feeling of release.

Our Universe is alive with a constant ebb and flow of "yin and yang," or "positive and negative" energies. There's no doubt about it—a master magician who has studied the Laws of Nature knows how to both heal and hex and they follow their own instincts in whatever their choice of magical action. Just as there are great benefits for all of us in the ever-changing seasons—the flow between night and day, summer and winter—there are also great benefits to be gained from embracing both your light-hearted and "bright goddess" nature, as well as loving your strong, assertive, and "dark goddess" nature. But there is no point in embracing all that you are and never using it to help yourself or others.

The universe doesn't put your magic into "positive" or "negative" categories. That is what your own free will and instincts are for—to give you a choice and the ability to make your own judgments.

But there is a long, illustrious history of respected Craft healers who use natural energy to release and resolve shadows of past hurts and, of course, to protect the more sensitive souls.

Once you start shedding some "light" on your inner self and feel that your instincts are honed and ready, you will gain a more complete sense of your own magic and learn to love all aspects of your own nature, including bringing some healing energy in and out of the shadows. Because the secret to it all is knowing that your intent is like a guiding light—it's a super jet that carries your magic to its purpose.

CHAPTER FOUR

Hex or Text?

Rituals, magic spells, and hexes of all kinds are creative events that can be as overtly ceremonial and theatrical or as simple and direct as the practitioner desires them to be.

Whatever style of ceremony is used, a spell needs to be as workable in the physical world as it is in the metaphysical.

So all kinds of methodologies can be used, including technology, the internet, and texts!

I like to use a combination of sorcery techniques depending on what type of spell I intend to cast, but I always take into account what environment I'm in as this will directly affect the methods and ingredients I can work with.

For example I might want to work some magic during a long flight from one city or one country to another, or I might be in the middle of nowhere with no access to any tools except my own body and mind, the earth firm beneath my feet, and the heavens soaring above me!

These days, the impulse to text can be overwhelming—and all of us have at one point or another been stung by someone's thoughtless text (or tweet!). But what you must keep in mind when spellcasting is that intent is everything.

Not only does a magic spell work by "intent" and the power of your thoughts—it is also helped with the alignment of your body, mind, and spirit. All "three" aspects of yourself can be brought together by

1. deep breathing and meditation,

2. letting go of nervous desire and impatience,

3. being consciously aware of your connection to the Eternal Universe .

All aspects of the Universe, including you, your mind, body, and spirit are connected—we are all energy. Everything we see around us is the physical manifestation of thought, and your thoughts have the power to change the atmosphere of your mind, which in turn can change the dynamic of the atmosphere around you.

Nothing is ever destroyed or disappears entirely; everything is energy and energy can only be transformed.

Before a spell is cast, it is preferable to create the right environment within and around you to "cleanse" your aura and the space or room you will be using for spellcasting. This can be done very simply by spending some quiet time alone, calming your energies by meditation and deep breathing, or, if possible, you can bathe or take a shower to help wash away built-up stress from the previous day's and evening's activities. If you're going to hex by text, turn your phone off, then on again. This clears stored-up negative electric charge—and gives you a minute or two to get your impulses under control!

When casting a magic spell, your own voice and words are one of the most important aspects to your ritual. Using your voice as a tool also triggers certain vibrations and resonance in the Universal atmosphere. The old Druids and Bards of the Celtic people considered poetry, music, and the spoken word to be full of great sorcery and spent many years honing their skills in wordcraft and songs. (Now you know why so many witches are creative artists, writers, and singers.) You can also learn to create your own minipoems and incantations by practicing your writing and artistry in this area.

CHAPTER FIVE

Let the Hexing Begin!

RESTING BITCHFACE

Backstabbing bitchy gossipers (especially ones with those kind of inscrutable faces who pretend to be your best friend) are a total pain in the neck.

You know—those troublemakers who suck up to you so they can get to hear your innermost secret thoughts and then, presto! These people will take great delight in going around town stirring up trouble and strife—revealing bits of your past and your most secret indiscretions.

Well, here is a spell an old wizard taught me that is just the ticket for hushing up loose lips and exposing those gossipers.

Ingredients

- 1 cup of salt

- Half a cup of red wine (the cheaper the better)

- A couple of nail clippings from the toe nails on your left foot (big toe will do)

- A leftover cooked chicken bone.

- Glass jar.

Instructions

Put all of the spell items into your cauldron, except the paper bag (if you don't have a witchy cauldron, just use an iron or aluminum soup pot).

Take the pot outside before the sun sets and stand under the sky. While stirring the mixture with a wooden spoon say this incantation out loud:

> *Stop this fraud and lying*
> *[. . . person's name . . .]*
>
> *Every fib and gossip you like*
> *to spread—*
> *will spin and turn to trip you up.*
>
> *Instead of me, you fill with dread—*
> *your cause will be to shut right up.*
>
> *Harm ye none—the fraud is over—*
> *If you try it again ye shall have no cover!*

Next, dump all the ingredients into the jar and then throw it away in a garbage bin.

HORRIBLE BOSS

You probably know this type of boss or workmate: hands and arms everywhere. The slimeball at work who, like an octopus with eight arms, just won't keep their clammy octo-hands to themselves.

To add to the insult, they are real sneaky and nobody else seems to have noticed what's happening to you.

Well this spell can help expose the freak while giving you the inner strength to speak out to the authorities and confront the abuser.

As a magical bonus it can also compel the harasser to reveal their true nature to all and sundry.

Spell time

The best time to cast this spell in order to reveal his (or her) inner octo traits is Saturday (the day of planet Saturn).

Ingredients

- Piece of paper (with the person's name written on it)

- A garlic clove (or one teaspoon of garlic paste)

- Half glass of filtered or mineral water.

- A teaspoon of cod liver oil (great for fishy spells)

- A feather (yellow or black, but any type will do)

- An empty screw top jar (such as a clean, empty jam jar)

- Opaque paper or plastic bag

Instructions

Place all your ingredients, except the bag into the jar and firmly twist on the lid. Then shake it for a moment while you say this incantation out loud:

With this elixir I now declare,
that it shall repel the octopus and the reveal the lecher,
with the best intentions and for my welfare,
if you touch me again, retribution shall be here.

Then wrap up the jar in the bag, and take it to work with you in your normal purse or briefcase. At some point during the day, walk just once around your desk/workstation in a counterclockwise direction while carrying the bag. You can leave it inside your purse or briefcase to avoid being too obvious if you like.

Finally, take the jar home with you at the end of the day and bury it in the ground somewhere in your yard or in a potted plant you keep in your balcony or courtyard. Leave it in the ground or potted plant until the spell has worked its purpose. Afterward you can dispose of the jar in a garbage can.

Revel in the knowledge that soon the abuser's true nature will be revealed.

JINX OFF

If your wish is to get rid of a jinx, or when you think something or someone is sending you shadowy bad vibes, then cast this spell at midday on any Sunday of the month.

Spell time

At noon any day or on a Sunday afternoon.

Ingredients

- Fresh ginger root or one teaspoon bottled ginger

- Some seaweed (straight from the sea if possible, but you can also use a Japanese nori roll or sushi paper)

- Any kind of water (pond, lake, or a bathtub full of water and sprinkled with salt)

Instructions

Stand near the water holding the ginger and either the nori paper or fresh seaweed in your right hand.

Breathe calmly and relax for a minute while focusing on peaceful and serene thoughts. As you gaze into the water, repeat this incantation:

> *By the gods of the wind and seed, ill wind and conflict is banished and sent far away from me.*

Next, throw the ginger and the nori paper into the water, then close your eyes and imagine that you are strolling along a beach, a warm breeze blowing through your hair. Imagine you are having a great time, feeling completely refreshed and untroubled and free of worries.

Wind up the final power of the spell by saying with confidence and conviction in your voice:

> *Now I see reflected only serenity and affection.*
> *And so it is, it is so, and so mote it be.*

TROLL STALKER

Some creep has been following you around or stalking you online.

Chill out and stay calm; you can rid yourself of this virtual pest with just a little help from the witchy world's favorite feline companion.

Apart from all the obvious protections you can do, like making sure people close to you know about it, and using your good sense—magically inclined people should be just as logical as everyone else—this ritual helps give a backup to any practical antistalking steps you are now going to take.

The side effects?

The only visible effects are fits of laughter when you think about this spell—and the occasional coughing up of fur balls (the troll not you).

Spell time

Weave this spell on a Saturday or the night of a full moon.

Ingredients

- A cat (your own or a friend's)

- A piece of brown paper (from a grocery bag is fine)

- Black pen

- Some clean kitty litter

- A litter tray

Instructions

Write the creepy stalker's name (or the word troll/stalker) on the paper with the pen and place it into the litter tray. Pour the kitty litter on top to cover everything

Next, wait for the cat to use the litter tray as normal.

When the tray is full, throw the dirty litter and paper in the garbage.

The tray can be put back to normal use by washing it out with warm, soapy water.

And make sure you pat good little kitty as a thank you for a job well done.

DIRTY ROTTEN SCOUNDREL

When you *just know* there is a traitor in your midst. Something is rotten in the state of Denmark, but you just cannot put your finger on who is the two-faced rotten egg.

The truth may hurt, but if there is disloyalty around, it really is better to know.

Spell time

To help you expose spies and disloyalty, cast this spell on the first or the last Saturday of any month and watch the rat run out of the bag.

Outdoors is best for this, but if you can't go outside, make sure you hang the clothesline near a window to capture the moon's energy.

Ingredients

- Photographs of any people you suspect (downloaded website pics, printed social media photos, etc).

- Wooden clothes peg

- Clothesline

- Black pepper shaker

Take the photographs and sprinkle black pepper over them, then pin them onto the clothesline with the wooden pegs.

Leave them there until the wind, rain, and elements dissolve the photos.

As the photos dissolve, so too will their desire to hurt and malign you be dissolved—a noble outcome if ever there was one!

BLACK DOGGONE

In many cultures there is the superstition that having a black cat cross your path is a sign of bad luck coming your way. But did you also know that the image of the black dog is also a powerful symbol of sorcery? The iconic image of a dog is used in many ancient Egyptian hexes, and still today the term "black dog" is often used to describe being gripped in a state of depression and fear.

But there is a way of turning that ancient superstition around on its dark furry head by allowing you to use that energy for your protection, to banish enemies, and to lift the veil of depression.

Let's show you how to have the power of the lucky dog on your side instead.

Spell time

An hour or so before the sun sets, gather the following items of magic.

Ingredients

- Two teaspoons of vegetable oil

- One teaspoon of any type of alcohol or wine

- A mixing bottle

- Some strands of hair from a black dog (if you can't get any, a photo of any dark-colored mutt will do)

- A white candle

Instructions

Pour the vegetable oil in the mixing bottle and add the alcohol.

Then pick up the bottle with both hands and warm it with the palms of your hands while you visualize a golden light of energy flowing into the bottle and into your hands and arms.

Do this until you feel positive energy flowing into your magical bottle as well—usually this takes a minute or so—and then sit down next to a table or bench where you have placed the hair or photo of the dog and the candle.

Place the bottle near the other magical items and light the candle.

Breathe deeply in and out a few times while you now hold the strands of hair or photo in your hands. In your mind's eye, visualize any fears, worries, and negative energy flowing away from your mind and body as positive golden light replaces it.

When you are ready, put a few drops of the magically infused oil on your fingertips and anoint the bottom of the candle and the hair or photo with it while concentrating on making your spell manifest.

As you do so, repeat:

Candle's power and lucky dog,
Please change my luck, so that I achieve
my heart's desire,
Powered by this magic fire.
And let it be done, that it harm no one.

To end the incantation, snuff or blow out the candle and place the dog's hair or photo and the magical oil bottle (with a stopper to keep it from leaking) somewhere private until you feel like you need to redo the spell as a booster.

DRUID'S LADDER

Do you deserve to step up the ladder at work but someone keeps sabotaging you?

The go-getters in life leave no stone (or twig) unturned when it comes to getting what they want, including stepping over you. There is no reason you can't do the same.

Trees, wood, and stones have played a significant part in magic-making for many thousands of years and especially during the times of the Druids in Europe. If you live near a park or can find a private area full of trees, that's great, but if not, any pieces of wood or branch that you find or buy will do.

Ingredients

- 3 fallen twigs or small pieces of pine about a foot long and a few inches wide

- A roll of string or natural rope

- A pen knife or a black marker pen

Instructions

Take your items of sorcery outside on a clear day where you won't be disturbed, or sit near an open window at home.

Think of what you want to overcome with this spell as you "climb up" your Druid's ladder. Is it a person's name you want to put there, since they are an obstacle to your success? Is it perhaps your own fear and inhibitions?

Really think about what is stopping you achieve your goal for next-level success and either carve it or write it onto one of the pieces of wood.

On the other 2 pieces of wood, carve or write these words.

Willow and rope
climb to hope.

Then tie the three pieces of wood together. (If you went to scout's training and know how to tie it to look like a small ladder, great, but otherwise know that the spell's power is just as potent by binding the three pieces of wood with string or rope and tying it off in a knot at the end to keep it bunched up together.)

When that is done, think about one goal at a time while you touch the ladder and say these enchanted words out loud:

By this wooden ladder I climb up to my success.
And it will be so,
Those who do not deserve to climb shall be overlooked
I step over the obstacle and this is my role
I deserve success and will gain my goal
Let it be done now with no negative emotion,
So Be It

To the end the incantation, breathe deeply a few times till you feel calm.

Keep the Druid's ladder and store it in a private space, a cupboard, or a garage.

Take it out, and think about any object, person, or fear that is sabotaging your chances. Whenever you feel the ladder's charms, you can strengthen the ladder's potency.

DRAGON SLAYER

Before you go out to a court appearance or to meet up with a tough competitor who is not on your side, get dressed in what you are going to be wearing for the meeting, and place your magical items on a table or ledge near you.

Ingredients

- A cup of cold ginger tea or glass of ginger beer

- Purple or blue candle

- A teaspoon of salt

Instructions

Light the candle and sprinkle the salt around yourself in a clockwise circle and say,

With the fire of the dragon I now burn away any fear
and opposition to my cause.
Dragon to dragon, magic to magic, we are equal.

Then sprinkle the salt in a counterclockwise direction around you and say out loud,

> *I am the light of the dragon*
> *watch me soar*
> *I feel the spirit of the dragon*
> *hear me roar*

Spread your arms out and feel yourself fly and soar and then let out a roar of a dragon.

And then take a sip of the ginger liquid, snuff or blow out the candle and whisper

> *so be it so.*

STILETTO SHADE

Some occasions call for a modern spell using ancient techniques and the latest fashion.

This is the perfect spell for feisty fashionistas.

Use this spell whenever you are getting the vibes that someone is either consciously or unconsciously passing on their shadows into your space, or whenever you are getting an uneasy feeling after you've been in someone's company. Or perhaps you feel heavy shadows following you after someone sends you a disturbing email.

Spell time

During a waning (diminishing moon) at midnight, perform this spell in a private area where you will not be disturbed.

Ingredients

• For women: a pair of red or black stiletto heels (the highest heels you can stand in)

- For men: heels would be nice, but you can wear a pair of heeled boots (cowboy boots are good for this)

- A photo of the suspect who is passing on the shadowy shade. If you don't have a photograph, then write down the name of the shady person on a piece of paper.

Instructions

Undress so you can be in sky-clad state, put on your high heels, and stand in front of a mirror alone.

Pick up the photo or piece of paper and put it on the floor in front of a mirror and stand with your legs apart over the paper or photo. Look at yourself in the mirror.

Then say out loud:

To be scorned by your shadow is not my role. Now as I name you I return your shade back to you as is my right. And from this night it's my shadow self you will view if mischief is your intended goal.

This shadow is released from me, and may it turn and serve you in the name of return and good will.

GET BACK, GET BACK
(Where you Belong)

When someone is really in your way and causing you problems either in your romantic relationships or any other circumstance, this is a great banishing charm to help get them back where they belong.

Spell time

Best time to cast is either on a Saturday or during a waning, diminishing moon phase.

Ingredients

- A purple candle
- Either a shaving or makeup mirror
- A red lipstick, or a red or purple crayon
- Some spring or mineral water

Instructions

Gather all your magical ingredients, and find a quiet place where you can be alone to cast this banishing charm.

Think of the name of the person you desire to get out of your way, and say their name out loud seven times.

Then pick up the mirror and, with the lipstick or crayon, draw a star shape onto the reflective surface.

Once you've done that, light the purple candle and look directly into the mirror, then repeat these magical words:

> *I call to thee goddess of heaven,*
> *to hear me now from one to seven.*
> *Magic Mirror reflect what I say and send*
> *any who wish us harm now out of our way.*
> *I cast this spell in the name of truth, it shall be done,*
> *So shall it be.*

Then blow or snuff out the candle. (If you wish, you may keep the candle in a safe place and re-use it again for other banishing spells.)

Next, carefully, so as not to smudge the star drawing, leave the mirror where it won't be disturbed for seven nights, like a cupboard or under a table.

Finally, at the end of the seven days and nights, pick up the mirror and wipe the star shape off the surface with a white cloth that has been soaked in the water, then say:

> *The spell has been cast, the magic will last,*
> *so mote it be*

You can then relax—going about your everyday life—and let the magical energy do its job.

HEX IN THE CITY

When city life gets you down with all the pressures of urban living, this is just the ritual to help you get away from the angst of heavy traffic, stifling crowds, and soaring prices.

Spell time

The best time is on a Saturday, the day of release and banishing. Pick any hour of the day that you can be alone.

Ingredients

- Half a cup of spring or filtered water
- One stick sandalwood incense and lighter
- A bottle of vanilla essence
- Three seeds from an orange
- A clean empty bottle with a lid

Instructions

Light the incense and sit nearby, breathing calmly and sensing the aroma of the sandalwood.

Take the empty bottle and drop in the orange seeds and three drops of vanilla essence and some of the water and put on the lid.

Hold the bottle in both hands, and picture yourself flying over the city rooftops, soaring with joy and freedom while you shake the bottle gently and say these words:

> *I shake the bottle to spread the energies*
> *I shake the bottle to soothe away my worries,*
> *I shake away the pressure and stress*
> *and now soar over this city with success.*

THAT VOODOO YOU DO

There are a growing number of wannabe social media divas, people who have thousands of followers but who are losing real friends and seem to be becoming as shallow as an empty martini glass. They even could have been a friend of yours once, but now it seems the only way to get this person's attention is to talk about them and *only* them by posting on their Instagram. Quick!

Do the girl/boy (and the rest of us) a big favor! For their sake and for the "good of all," it's time to brew up this "Hey babe, what's going on with your hair in that last post?" charm.

This charm is totally harmless and lasts only for one day.

Ingredients

- A secondhand doll (Barbie dolls are collectors' items now, so you may want to use anything else, as long as no one wants it anymore)

- 1 teaspoon of salt

- A few strands of dog hair

- A mirror

- A glass of filtered or spring water

Instructions

Find a quiet space where you can perform your magic ritual and place all your ingredients on a table or the floor.

Begin your spell by sprinkling the salt in a circle on the floor around you in a clockwise direction.

Next, hold the doll in both hands and say:

> *I cast this spell in the name of good,*
> *no harm will be done, 0 blessed Be.*

Next, stick the dog hair onto the head of the doll with the glue and let it dry for a few moments.

Then take the doll and sit on the floor inside the circle of salt. Meditate for a few moments and then say:

> *Just for today, just for a day,*
> *when you look in the mirror you will see* your true way.

> *Step back from your self and look into the light,*
> *the hair is a mess, but your soul will be right.*

Now place the doll in front of a mirror, and think about the person you wish to have a bad-hair day while you mess up the doll's hair into knots. Once your antihairstyling is achieved, leave the doll as is all night and also the following day.

Then about twenty-four hours later, take the doll and dust it over with a pinch of the salt, which will help clear the energy again. Following that, give the doll's hair a quick wash in some spring water, comb and towel dry, and there you have it—now the doll and the vanity diva is on the way to finding their true self once more.

FELINE FAKERY

No one appreciates having aspects of their identity being faked by anyone, let alone by friends or family. People may tell you that mimicry is a form of flattery, but it soon gets old having someone else trying to copy your individual ideas, your style, or even trying to steal your name and identity.

Apart from trademarking your brand names and work, you can also magically protect yourself from copycats by writing your ideas and any name or brand you need to protect on a piece of white paper with a blue pen. In your mind's eye, visualize a globe of white light surrounding you and the page in front of you.

Next, visualize the light as a protective power sending sparks of magnetic force within and without, and say these words:

Vanity and fakery is not pure art.
Morality is in the higher form of my heart,
Others may try to copy me but for my sake
they are seen as FAKE!

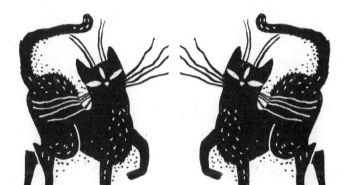

FREEZE FRAME

This spell is to be used when you are completely fed up with someone's awful behavior and they just keep popping up in your life when you don't want them anywhere near you. It won't hurt anyone; it just helps them make up their mind to leave you alone.

Get an ice tray and fill it with cold water.

Either write down the person's name who is harassing you or find a photo of them alone.

Put the piece of paper or photo in a small ziplock bag, getting most of the air out before closing. Then place the bag inside the ice tray and set the tray in the freezer (preferably where it wont be disturbed by other people).

Once it is frozen, and if you prefer it to remain frozen, you can wrap it in brown or white paper so it won't be disturbed or looked at by other people.

Do this spell with positivity, feeling confident in your ability to speak your mind and defend yourself whenever needed.

Keep it in the freezer until you have your desired result, then throw in the trash.

CHAPTER SIX

Get Your Power Back

VROOM VROOM BROOM

There are some ancient recipes for "flying pomades," which were used for broomsticks, but since we are modern sorcerers, we much prefer traveling by jet. I use this spell whenever I want to get a good seat on a plane, but you can also use it for attracting a job in aviation.

Ingredients

- A small bowl
- 1 teaspoon of jojoba oil
- 1 teaspoon of sunflower oil
- 2 drops of jasmine essential oil
- A silver spoon
- 1 chicken stock cube
- A clean jar with a lid

Instructions

On the night of a full moon, mix together in the bowl the jojoba and sunflower oils and jasmine essential oil with the silver spoon as you concentrate on seeing yourself happily sitting in your favorite seat on the plane or leading the crew in the first-class cabin, and repeat this incantation:

> *Silver of Mercury my night-time Sun,*
> *in Moonlight's power enchantment has begun.*

Then crumble half the stock cube and sprinkle a little bit into the oil as you say:

Birds of a feather, I call thee nigh!
With Magic's touch I will soon fly.

Wipe a tiny bit of the ointment behind your knees and keep the rest of it in the jar.

BITCHY BREW

A great potion for yourself when you want to feel strong but without any bitchy side effects.

Ingredients

- A slice of lemon

- 1 teaspoon of orange marmalade

- 2 cups of hot water

- 1 teaspoon of fresh mint or dried mint for tea

- 1 teaspoon of dried chamomile for tea

- Hot water

Place all the ingredients in a teapot and pour in the hot water. Allow the brew to sit for 5 minutes as you repeat this incantation:

Earth, Fire, Air, and Sea, Natural Magic come to me.

BAD HABIT BANSHEE

This spell works like a charm to get rid of any bad habits like smoking, alcohol, or drug abuse, or unwanted yearnings for an abusive ex-partner.*

Ingredients

- A cup
- A white candle
- Sandalwood incense
- An empty cup

Instructions

Set the empty cup on a table in front of the candle. Light the incense and the candle, and stand near the table as you pick up the cup in both hands and hold it high over the candle and incense. Breathe slowly and evenly for a moment until you are calm and centered. Then hold the cup near your chest and slowly blow air into it, silently naming each bad habit and negative energy you wish removed from your life. When finished, turn the cup upside down onto the table, saying firmly:

The contents of this vessel, I give up to thee, Lords of Light, exchange these bad habits for positive actions.

Finish by blowing out the candle and incense and saying:

It shall be done, O Blessed be.

*This spell is not meant to be a panacea for serious issues. If you are in a dangerous relationship, feel unsafe, or suffer from addiction, seek professional help at once!

MIRROR MIRROR

You know that old superstition—if you break a mirror, then seven years bad luck—well this ritual will reverse the so-called curse and get you shining in front of your own reflection in no time.

So sweep the pieces of your broken mirror into a pile, sprinkle salt and rosemary over the pieces, scoop them up carefully with a pan and small broom while wearing gloves, and throw them into the garbage bin.

Then light a stick of sandalwood incense stick and walk counterclockwise around the bin seven times as you say:

One year gone of bad luck,
now two, three, four, five, six, and seven.

Then walk clockwise around the bin as you say:

Powers of the Universe, bring good fortune for one year,
and two, three, four, five, six, and seven. So Be It.

TOTALLY OVER IT

There are times when no matter how hard you try, no matter how much you do to save a relationship, no matter how much you forgive and forget what they did to you, sometimes you really need cosmic assistance to help a bad love fade away.

And this is just one of those kinds of spells. So now that you've completely made up your mind it's *over*, gather the following spell items.

Ingredients

- A purple candle in a candlestick holder

- A silver candle in candlestick holder

- A half a cup of salt

- A mugwort smudge stick or mugwort incense

- Some matches or a lighter

- A piece of brown paper

- A pencil

- A glass or china bowl of either filtered or spring water

Instructions

Place everything on a table or a flat surface in a private place where you will not be interrupted by anyone or anything.

Place the paper flat on the table and write the (soon-to-be) ex's name on the left side of the paper and your name on the right side. In the space between each separate name, draw a straight vertical line down the middle.

Place the silver candle in the candlestick holder in front of the paper to represent good intention, so as to harm none. This reinforces the fact that you simply want closure from this relationship and the contact with them to end—as well as any bad feelings on either side to fade away.

Now place the purple candle in the candlestick holder behind the silver one. The purple candle symbolizes finality—which is what you desire from this spell.

When you light both candles, it will signify the element of fire. And when you light the mugwort incense stick, which is renowned for helping dreams take flight, it will represent the element of Air.

The cup of water is, of course, the Water element, and the salt that you will dust around you in a counterclockwise direction (from left to right), signifies the Earth element.

Now hold some of the salt in your left hand and moving to the left, cast the circle by sprinkling the salt around the table in a full circle of magical banishing.

Light the mugwort and walk clockwise (to the right) completely around the table, waving the smoke from the mugwort around you. Then place it on the table (on a china or metal plate) where it can continue to infuse the cleansing smudge smoke, gently and safely.

Next, pick up the paper on which you've written both names and tear it in half along the vertical line so the name of your ex is one side and your name is on the other. You now have two pieces of paper.

Take the paper with your ex's name, light it with the purple candle, and quickly put it in the bowl of water. Leave it there all night, then, in the morning, pour the water and paper into a hole you have dug in the ground, and cover with soil.

On the same evening you do this spell, take the other side of paper with your name and put it in a drawer in your bedroom where you keep your most precious items. Leave it there until the spell works or as long as you like.

At the end of the spellcasting that evening, make sure to snuff out the candles; snuff out and discard the mugwort by putting one end in the water and throwing it all away.

ROAD RESCUE PARFUM

Awful people are driving all the time—and this is one of those times when you don't want something bad to happen to this awful person! This particular spell falls in the category of personal power: you need some soothing self-control in this instance.

Perfumes, since ancient times, have had dual purposes. Not only are they produced for attracting lustful thoughts (or hiding the pungent odor of the great unwashed), but there are other, more secret purposes for those in the know. Following, one such alternate purpose and recipe is revealed.

Even in times of chariots and horse-driven carts, lane hoggers and road-rage drivers were just as prevalent as they are now. So what to do? Simple: prepare your vehicle and your own body with some rescue parfum that will be sure to soothe and protect you from any savage road-hogging beast.

Sspell time

Begin infusing this pleasantly scented parfum oil with magical properties sometime during a new or full moon.

Ingredients

- 3 teaspoons of coconut oil

- 3 drops of vanilla essence

- 2 drops of orange or mandarin essential oil

- A pinch of dried rose or your favorite dried flower

Instructions

Soften the coconut oil by leaving it near a sunny window or warm area. Mix all ingredients together with a wooden spoon in a glass bowl while you charge the formula with magic by saying,

I charge these oils by the Sun and Moon
to drive away anger or fear.
Wherever I place them bring perfumed tranquility,
O blessed be.

Then spoon the mixture into small clean jar and firmly screw on the lid. Keep the jar in your car or bag and dab a small amount of this rescue parfum on pulse points whenever needed.

DARK SIDE MOON TONIC

It's little known that not only is reflective moonlight powerful, but also the dark moon energy can infuse your charms with stunning glamor power.

Spell time

On the night of a waning, diminishing moon

Ingredients

- A crystal or smooth stone

- A glass

- Some spring or mineral water

Instructions

Put a crystal or a smooth stone into a glass and fill it up with either spring or mineral water.

Once night has fallen and before midnight, place the glass outside or near a window so that the moon's rays can charge both the crystal and the water.

Leave it there all night long where no one will stumble over it or knock it over.

The next morning when you awaken, gather up the glass and hold it up in both hands, saying

Goddess Luna, I thank you,
Goddess Sun now I go to meet you.

Both the crystal and the water are now filled with maximum lunar potency. So take out the crystal and keep it with your precious items or magical tools because this moon-charged crystal can help you with lots of banishing and protection spells.

The water has also been charged with moon energy, and you should pour this into a glass container with a lid and use it when you want to sprinkle it over an item to protect it or use it for one of the banishing spells in this book.

CHAPTER SEVEN

Instant Mojo

Need an instant mojo for a quick spell fix? So how is that done? There are many ways to create a fast-acting magical charm, and here are ten of my favorites using the power of color.

Just shake up a cup of minute mumbo to create an all-purpose talisman using color power, which is the perfect ingredient to add to build amulets and talismans.

RED

Has the just right abracadabra power to enhance passion, lust, energy, and vitality, and for hexing. Red can also conjure sorcery success against jealousy and those "psychic vampires" who can suck the energy out of you with their constant negativity.

This is how to make a mobile talisman, perfect when an ex-lover feels envious and can't let go, or you are getting jealousy vibes from your new partner's ex.

To instantly charge your talisman you will need:

- A red scarf or ribbon.

Clasp the red ribbon in your hand and spin it above your head in a clockwise direction. As you do, visualize the jealous rival or envious ex-lover and say out loud:

Love and success is what I need—but all I see
is just your jealousy,
Now may we spin like this ribbon
And make jealousy hidden
I will be so protected from all your envy.

ORANGE

Is full of the mojo of creativity, health, and for hexing use. The color orange is a great ingredient in spells to stop voodoo affecting you as well as gaining power over sicknesses like flu and fever that you could catch from other people.

The easiest talisman is to squeeze a fresh orange into juice in the morning to drink, then take another whole orange with you wrapped in tissue paper (don't eat this one—it is for absorbing flus and fevers).

When you come home from your day out, throw the orange in the bin and get a new one for the next day out during flu season.

Green

Is one of the most powerful colors of nature as well as a color for luck and growth.

For hexing, use green to grow your physical strength against an enemy.

At seven in the morning or seven at night, hold a piece of spinach and say these words,

> *Spinach Spinner, grow your strength*
> *and give me the power against my enemies and fears,*
>
> *So be it now, it is done!*

Always take something green with you when you feel a bit weak around others or are going into a dangerous or nerve-racking situation.

Yellow

Intense concentration, mental ability

For hexing, you can wear something yellow to help focus the intent of your spell and help you avoid psychic bounce backs.

Blue

Success, peace, tranquility, protection

For hexing, blue can be used in all spells of protection on its own or as an additional color of protective power and successful outcomes.

Purple

Spirituality, psychic ability, enchantment

For hexing, purple can be used in deeply spiritual protections and mojos. This color can give you extra enchanted power, especially if you like to use the energy of ancient gods and goddesses.

White

Truth, purity, meditation, spiritual protection

For hexing, white is an excellent all-round spiritual protection, and helps you and your intended magical recipient get to their inner truth.

Brown

Animal magic, environment, grounding

For hexing, brown is a powerful earthing color to keep you protected while spellcasting when you want to burn or bury a mojo pouch.

Gold

The sun, wealth, royalty

For hexing, gold is not used for avenging except for casting spells to return or gain money, and for protection and finding out where your money has been taken.

Silver

Mysticism, the moon, money

For hexing, silver is the perfect moon boosting ingredient, especially on the night of a new or full moon. This color will intensify any power spell for protection or avengement.

CHAPTER EIGHT

Psychic Protection

PAST-LIFE ORACLE SPINNER

To help you get a clearer view of past lives, cast this spell on the day of a new moon and repeat it once every week for a month.

Take a small white onion and soak it in a bowl of mineral water for half an hour and then take it out and dry it thoroughly with a clean cloth.

Meditate for a few minutes while you hold the onion in your hands and then start to peel off the first and second layers of the onion while you repeat this incantation:

> *Memories of the distant past,*
> *come forward into the light.*

Place the layers you have peeled off into a paper bag and bury near a tree. Keep the rest of the onion wrapped in the refrigerator to use again whenever you desire to look into this kind of magic "time machine" once more.

WIKIDISIMA

There are times when you must boost your inner warrior, and I have found that one of the best ways is to connect with the inner energy I call the "Wikidisima," pronounced "wicked-is-ima" (for female power) or "Wikidisimo" (for male power).

Rise early on a Sunday morning and cast this spell before you begin your daily routine.

Take a refreshing shower using an aloe body gel and a firm sponge or loofah to slough off any dull and dry skin from your body.

Stand under the warm water while you wash away all of your fears and weakness. Feel yourself being filled with new strength and vigor.

When you are ready, wrap yourself in a freshly washed towel and look into your bathroom mirror as you say:

I feel my eternal power
There's nothing I cannot achieve,
no path I cannot travel, no barrier to my success.
Rise within me, my warrior, my Wikidisima/o.

KARMA QUEEN

We often forget to look after our spiritual and psychic nature, and this spell can help align you with the universe and karmic energies around you.

Ingredients

- a clear quartz crystal
- red henna powder or non-toxic red, water-based paint
- a small paintbrush

Instructions

Find some time to be alone and undisturbed for at least half an hour, and dress in some comfortable, light-colored clothing. Using the paintbrush, apply a small red dot to your third eye chakra (in the middle of your forehead), and also paint a dot in the center palm of each of your hands. Sit cross-legged on the floor while you hold the crystal in your two hands, and breathe calmly and deeply while you meditate and let go of thoughts of daily stresses and worries. Next, repeat this incantation:

Thank you, oh cosmos, for my awareness of
the eternal power of spirit.
I open my psychic mind to the Karma Queen.

SOUL PROTECTOR

Take some time for your soul to recover from hurt and pain with this spiritually protective, self-care booster.

On the day of a full or waxing moon, revive your aura by burning some orange or sandalwood incense and dressing in some white or purple clothing.

Sit in front of an open window and breathe in and out deeply for a few moments to calm your body and mind.

Rest your hands on your knees with your palms facing upwards and repeat this incantation:

*Deep within me. I shall put away my fears and know
that I deserve to fulfil my dreams and follow my true purpose.
I open my mind and soul in the flow of my universal goal.*

So mote it Be.

DREAM FINDER

The ancient occultists understood that "when the body sleeps, the soul awakens," and that our dreams are a magical source of creativity, insight and divination.

Dreams are just like secret messages from our spiritual soul. They give us information on what is really happening deep in our subconscious mind and the universe around us.

With these dream spells and enchanted rituals you can also learn to tap into the power of your dreams—to show you how to best deal with everyday troubles and to give you important insights into the past and the future.

We can all learn how to remember our dreams more clearly by following these mind-power and focusing techniques.

First, make sure that you go to sleep in a quiet environment, without the interference or distraction of outside noises. If you do fall asleep while watching TV or listening to music, your dreaming pattern will take on some of what you have seen and heard and will not be a real insight into your subconscious.

Start a Dream Workbook. Put a new diary and pen near your bed and as soon as you wake up in the morning, write down immediately any images or emotions you had while you slept.

Before you go to sleep, sit on your bed and breathe calmly and deeply for a moment or two to relax, and then repeat this incantation:

> *Peace and understanding flow this night,*
> *O Universe, let me remember my dreams*
> *and clear my second sight.*

SLEEPY SOLUTIONS

You know that old saying "Go and sleep on it"?

Well, it is true that while we sleep, we can call on our higher wisdom to help make big decisions and solve all sorts of problems.

To do this, before you go to bed, write your problem or question on a piece of red paper.

Sit in a quiet place, hold the paper in front of you, and gaze at the color of the paper and the words you have written. Don't think about your problem or anything else; relax your mind, and let yourself absorb the warmth and vibrancy of the color.

Then, just before you lie down, tear the paper into pieces and sprinkle them and some chamomile tea leaves under your bed.

In the morning you will start to feel an answer to your important question forming. An old Celtic charm for insightful dreams is to sprinkle salt under the four corners of the bed, and walk clockwise around your bedroom three times with your question in mind.

NIGHTMARE ON MAIN STREET

A magic potion to guard against nightmares can be made by mixing a teaspoon of apple-cider vinegar and a teaspoon of honey into a small cup of warm water and sipping this elixir slowly before bedtime.

PSYCHIC VAMPIRES

Whenever you have dreams about being chased, it is often your intuition warning you of those people in your life (whether known or unknown) who are trying to use your energy—literally suck up your life force. You'll know who they are after you get off the phone with them or see them face to face; you will feel as if you are mentally and physically drained.

You need to face these psychic vampires in order to get rid of them. This is done by "programming" yourself to stop running in your dreams. Tell yourself as you prepare to fall asleep that you are courageous, and tonight you will actually turn around to face whoever or whatever is chasing you.

You will find that your inner strength will now come out to fight those fears, plus any vampiric energy from fair-weather friends will dissolve in front of your eyes during your dreams and waking hours.

VIEWING THE FUTURE

To evoke dreams of future gazing and prediction, wear an amethyst crystal or moonstone on a chain or leather strap around your neck at night.

CHAPTER NINE

The Shady Side of the Zodiac

Sometimes the best defense against people with awful behavior is native to the person themselves. Were they born that way? Have they developed a personal vendetta against you or are they simply living up to the worst qualities of their own sun sign?

In other words, maybe they can't really see what they are doing that seems wrong in your eyes, and you shouldn't take it too personally—it's already in their star-crossed nature!

But that doesn't mean you have to put up with their negativity toward you. Whatever the reason, when you are having trouble with someone and in order to take stock of the situation, it's advisable to look at tools and techniques like these zodiac-inspired tips to help you get down to the astro-roots of the matter. Once you have a sense of what makes them tick, you can choose your spells accordingly.

Then, whenever you are stumped by someone's negativity, you can learn to turn the tables by recognizing what is going on and know instantly how to play that game right back at them.

ARIES

On the whole, Aries folk can be charismatic, funny, and loyal to their closest friends and loved ones. But if you are having trouble understanding the actions of a certain Aries person, then you have likely come across their shady side, which is the "me–me" mindset. In certain situations, Aries can become completely self-centered and immature. They often will say out loud whatever is on their minds without thinking first and can really hurt you with a sting of their sharp tongue and careless words.

Aries are natural pranksters and make good comedians, but this flippant manner often hides many deeply held fears. They prefer to make light of any hidden parts of their lives that threaten their equilibrium rather than deal with them sensibly to gain life experience.

Aries are known to be hot-headed and impatient, so you need to hone your quick wit and have handy a few comeback lines to beat them at their own game!

TAURUS

Taureans are great appreciators of beauty. On the positive side they can see and produce loveliness in others and themselves.

And then there's vanity: checking out their own reflection is common for Taureans, whether they are good looking in the film-star sense or not. Through hard knocks the world can bring, they often develop a strong sense of self-love for their own survival, which can make it very hard for anyone to find a space in their heart. Being weak-willed, overdoing it on food and drink is common for Taurus. The bull sign also needs constant encouragement to stop avoiding work deadlines because they are natural procrastinators.

A final word of advice is to be careful not to stir anger in a sleeping bull without safety measures in place; their tempers are legendary.

GEMINI

Chameleon of the stars, Gemini is very clever, but their negative side inclines them toward gossip. They can speak and write about things that can cause blowups, and although not intentional, can deeply hurt others.

They have that twin factor, which can be used for goodness and a bit of wickedness thrown in. They are verbal volcanoes waiting to blow up. When they get on a high horse there is no way to shut them up; they can be gossipers and fall into minutia and trivia. They are sometimes tricky and deceitful in their attempts to get what they want. They can also be obsessively jealous and surprisingly vindictive if they get the feeling others are working behind the scenes against them.

Your best defense against this is to keep cool and never get in the middle of a gossip fest with them about other people.

Of course, don't tell them your deepest secrets as you can bet they will release any information when it's useful for their own benefit.

CANCER

When these moon people are fond of you and showing their best face, they are among the most loving, supportive, and surprisingly intuitive friends or lovers you can have on your side.

But all of us have a shady area lurking back there somewhere. The shadow side of Cancer makes them prone to sudden irrationality when pushed too far or taken out of their comfort zone—especially during a full moon.

They love deeply and forever when they find "the one," but when heartbroken, they can plot revenge and never forget a perceived slight made against them.

There is certainly a dark side of the moon. Since Cancer is ruled so completely by moon dust, they can sometimes wallow in their own dark side and even want to hide in the shadow side for quite a while until something or someone drags them out.

LEO

Leo is a fascinating character. In fact, some of the most famous and richest celebrities are Leos. If you learn how to stroke their egos, scratch their sweet spot, and make sure they are (or let them think they are) on top of the pedestal where they can watch over their colony of admirers like the alpha feline in a lion's den, then you will be able to handle any kind of snarls and unwarranted outbursts from them.

You see, it's all because, zodiac-wise, Leo must always be number one—the boss—and they expect loyalty from their team.

They can be ruthlessly cold-blooded if it means they need to make a business decision and will often choose self-preservation and working solo over having to make compromises.

They are ruled by the sun, so be careful you don't get burned. Possibly the best way to handle them is with cool charm so their fiery temper doesn't prove too hot to handle.

VIRGO

Virgos will keep much of their lives private, and some have secret double lives that would surprise even their closest friends.

They are extremely complex and intense in their need for alone time and private thoughts.

They can suffer from black moods and depression due to pressures of the outside world; nervous natures, anxiety, and insomnia are common, so they will have plenty of time at night to lie in bed mulling over who and what has double-crossed them. Even though they may appear confident and in control of the smallest details of their lives, Virgos often feel insecure and may not feel confident enough to share all their thoughts and dreams with you or their closest friends and family.

Their fall-back tendency is to rely on their famous intellect, instead of their quite deeply felt emotional intuition. They may start telling fibs in order to keep you none the wiser.

Virgos never want to admit that they don't know the answer to everything—because they try their hardest to do just that!

LIBRA

Librans are very romantic in the sense of lighthearted fun but are not easy to pin down into a full-time relationship. They would be happy to stay if the honeymoon period remained forever, but we know that is impossible because real life for humans is not happiness all the time.

Libra will prefer to head for the hills rather than deal with heavier issues surrounding money problems or solutions and decisions on love and romantic partnerships.

They can be very selfish and quite lazy in dealing with problems, expecting others to do the dirty work for them. Librans often prefer others to take the lead and to make the hard decisions, particularly in committing to relationships.

Subconsciously, their efforts to balance their psychological scales between justice for everyone and their own self satisfaction can cause them to feel paralyzed by inaction. This can become very tiresome and frustrating for their loved ones and business partners.

SCORPIO

This should come with a warning sign: DON'T MESS WITH A SCORPIO. But there are ways to get them to take karmic responsibility for wrongdoings, just be careful how you do it and don't tell anyone they may know what's happening until it happens. Scorpios like to appear strong and their manner can be very charismatic, but this surface appeal often hides deep insecurities, which is handy for you to know.

They have to use their sting to stop people from seeing their vulnerable sides, which in their mind is a sign of weakness. Think twice before you lend a Scorpio money without a strong legal contract because they will never forgive you if you dare ask for the money back before they decide it's the right time to do so. Another faux pas against a Scorpio is letting anyone else know you had to help them out—you thought you were being kind but woe be tide if it gets out that they actually weren't perfect, sexy, and richly independent enough to never need a helping hand.

SAGITTARIUS

On guard! Once you hang around a Sagittarian long enough you get to realize that this optimistic, risk-taking travel-lover also has a shady side and—let's face it—everyone has one!

One of the most annoying traits a Sagittarian can have is their flakiness. They can be a bit superficial and are not known as one of the most responsible of the star signs. In other words, "heartbreaker" and "ghosting" are typical words that apply to those who haven't learned to control their dark urges.

They can also be self-absorbed and miss signals where some patience and time spent listening out for friends' problems would be the norm.

A Sagittarian can run a mile from responsibility and often wish they could gallop off without a word to some distant land where they feel the grass might be greener.

CAPRICORN

Capricorns are the moguls of the zodiac. Whether focusing on their own potential or actually fulfilling their dream, making money or gaining success in business is often a major driving force. Being around them, you can absorb the secrets of success and it is to your advantage to have a Capricorn somewhere in your business team or as a financial advisor.

But it will also be handy for you to know that the shadow side of this all-encompassing drive to succeed is that the energizer goat can also be a bit of a snob; they often judge people on their usefulness or whether they have the necessary prestige and good contacts with which to climb the mountain of achievement ahead. At their worst, goats can store up their own money and contacts and feel resentful in sharing the golden egg because they have had to work so hard on their own to build their own assets.

A good way to handle Capricorns is to show them you are prepared to add to their plans and not to take advantage or try to use their contacts.

AQUARIUS

Aquarius, the water carrier, needs a lot of space to be themselves both internally and externally. Because their minds are so expansive and their spirits need a sense of freedom, the negative side to all this universal head space is that their partners and friends can often feel neglected and have their needs ignored. The Aquarian dark side is usually involved in secretive or hidden traits; they may like to walk on the wild side while keeping these adventures away from their loved ones and business partners. They prefer to keep their worlds separate.

Despite having a great sense of the world in an intellectual and often spiritual way, this airy sign can be weirdly insensitive to others' feelings and without empathy when it is needed.

One of the most annoying traits of Aquarians is that they can be charismatic and a joy to be around, but then go missing when deep conversations about unpaid bills and future planning comes up. Sound familiar?

PISCES

This loving star can be one of the most fascinating people around. They often have wonderfully soulful eyes that you can dive into, making you feel like you are swimming through a luxurious pool of cool blue water.

They can often lead an entirely secret life in their own minds even if they don't act on it. Because of this, it would feel entirely natural for them to keep a side of themselves away from you, which is fine if you are not close, but if you had started making plans to be the couple of the year, it might prove a stumbling block. They are also prone to run like an athlete from responsibility and may drink or gamble to excess.

But when things go wrong, that water gets murky—so much so that you may not see where you're going. Well, if that happens to you, that's exactly the time you know you're experiencing some of that famous Pisces shade.

This aqua-person operates under planetary influences that are full of out-of-this-world fantasies and desires.

CHAPTER TEN

Spell Time, Moon Time

The tried and true method of magical timing is to match up a particular type of spell or ritual with the corresponding phase of the moon. Even the most skeptical of scientists knows that the moon directly affects not only the Earth's tides, but also our most basic animal and human emotions.

Waxing or Growing Moon

Use this time to attract magic toward you to grow prosperity. This period also gives you room to expand choices in careers and relationships. Good for strengthening and developing affairs of the heart and boosting commitment or marriage vows.

Full Moon

This is the premiere witchy time for any kind of sorcery but especially to hoist your intent up to the next level of power, like weaving charms to attract what you need and repel what you certainly don't need (or want).

Waning or Diminishing/Shrinking Moon

This time frame is ideal to finish a relationship or to banish negative energy; it gives the perfect opportunity to get rid of bad old love habits (like jealousy and nagging) and to well and truly get over an ex.

Dark Moon

And let's not forget the time of dark moon—certainly not a great time for attraction and new love spells (could be perfect for signing those longed-for divorce papers, though), but this is an excellent phase to let you take time out for little ol' you and reflect on what you would like in your life for the future. This will prepare you for a new beginning and the upcoming new moon.

New Moon

Use the new moon to get moving on new projects. It provides wonderful lunar energies to help kick-start jobs, projects, and finances, or to bring back passions and excitement into slightly frayed partnerships.

ABOUT THE AUTHOR

Deborah Gray is a bestselling Australian author who was born into a long heritage of Celtic magick and mysticism. Initiated as a teenager into an Ancient Druid Circle, she has studied magick and metaphysics for over twenty years, inheriting her knowledge of parapsychology and spellcasting from one of the world's few remaining Druid Masters. She is author and coauthor of six international bestsellers including *Nice Girl's Book of Naughty Spells*, *How to Turn Your Ex-Boyfriend into a Toad*, and *Spells for all Seasons*.

Deborah is one of her genre's best-known and respected writers. Her work has been translated into seven languages, and her lushly produced magical video series, "Wish on a Spell," continues to excite the imaginations of many thousands of people around the world.

Visit Deborah's website at *www.deborahgray.com*

HAMPTON ROADS PUBLISHING COMPANY

. . . for the evolving human spirit

Hampton Roads Publishing Company publishes books on
a variety of subjects, including spirituality, health,
and other related topics.

For a copy of our latest catalog, call (978) 465-0504 or visit
our distributor's website at *www.redwheelweiser.com*.
You can also sign up for our newsletter and special offers by
going to *www.redwheelweiser.com/newsletter*